GUITAR FOR I
THE COMPLETE SONGBOOK

Adrian Gavinson

ADRIAN GAVINSON

WELCOME

Welcome guitarists of all ages and abilities to this essential songbook. Each song is suitable for all levels from beginner to advanced. Try mastering them all and enjoy!

ADRIAN GAVINSON

SONGS

Swing Low, Sweet Chariot

This Little Light of Mine

I'll Fly Away

Danny Boy

Drunken Sailor

America The Beautiful

Home On the Range

I've Got Peace Like a River

Blue Christmas

Deck the Halls

Amazing Grace

Be Thou My Vision

Here I am Lord

BEGINNER GUITAR CHORDS

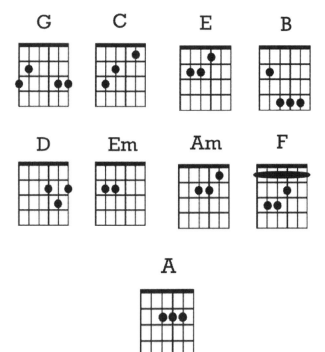

GUITAR FOR BEGINNERS
THE COMPLETE SONGBOOK

GETTING STARTED

Welcome to the beginner's guide to playing guitar. I know what you're thinking. You want to be the next Jimi Hendrix right? You want to be able to rock out on the guitar without instruction and freely navigate the fretboard. Well you will be able to with hard work and practice. And of course, a sound understanding of the world's most awesome instrument.

Before playing a single note though, we have to tune up. Tuning the guitar takes time and patience especially when starting out. With   months and years of experience, you'll be able to tune without the help of a tuner. Every song, exercise and riff in this book uses what we call **standard tuning**. Standard tuning is the basic guitar tuning that most players use. This is:

E   A   D   G   B   E

We tune the guitar from the low string (E) to the high string (E). The lowest E is the one nearest to you. This is also the thickest string. There are some great youtube videos with tuners which let you match the note. Alternatively, you could purchase a guitar tuner which fits on the headstock of the guitar and ready to go. However, in this day and age, it's more practical to just find a free tuner online and tune up before playing.

Now that you are in tune, let's take a look at the basics of the guitar. Getting to know your instrument is the most important step that you can take when beginning your guitar journey. This is for health and safety and also for the reason that when you understand the ins and outs of your instrument, you can proceed to having a better comprehension for how to get the best sound out of it.

On the page opposite, we have a diagram of an acoustic guitar with labels so that you can see what's what. Acoustic guitars are one of the three main guitar types: electric, acoustic and classical. Of course, hybrids of the instruments exist but traditionally, these are the three varieties.

headstock

fretboard

tuning pegs

sound hole

bridge

body

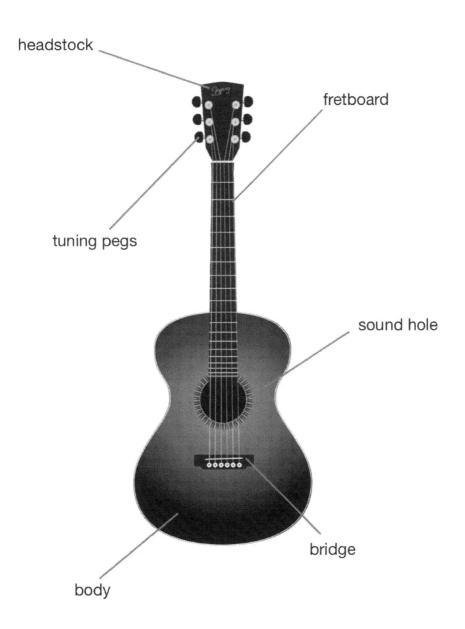

Here is a diagram of the acoustic guitar is all of her majesty.

Let us begin by exploring what each part of the instrument is for and the essence of what makes an acoustic guitar the versatile and amazing instrument that it is.

The first component labelled is the head-stock. This is where the brand of the guitar is typically found. The headstock has six pegs screwed in to it which are called tuning pegs. These are what we use to tune the gui-tar. Please note that this is a sensitive region and any damage done will permanently detriment the sound and playability of your guitar. It is best that you are careful and ensure to only touch this part of your instrument if you have to such as for tuning or tightening purposes.

Next is the fretboard. Acoustic guitars tend to have between 20 and 24 frets although there are many exceptions. Frets are the marked lined regions on the neck of the guitar. There are typically dots to help mark the 3rd, 5th, 7th, 9th, 12th, 15th, and 17th frets.

Following this, we have the sound hole. This is the distinguishing characteristic of an acoustic or classical guitar. The sound hole is the hole in the middle of the instrument where the sound comes out. On solid body electric guitars, there is no sound hole which means that when you play an electric guitar dry (that is, without plugging it in), hardly any sound escapes. The hole on acoustic guitars enables the guitar to resonate. Again, leave the sound hole alone for the most part.

A frustrating but surprisingly common mishap with acoustic guitarists is that they drop their pick inside of the guitar when playing. If this happens, do not do anything that could potentially cause damage to your instrument. Instead, turn the guitar upside down with the sound hole facing the floor. Lure the pick towards the hole by gently shaking the entire guitar with both hands firmly gripping the instrument. The pick will then fall out and therefore, mission accomplished.

The body of the guitar is self-explanatory. When you become more advanced on the guitar, you might be interested in learning about the different types of woods that are used to make the body and neck of the guitar and subsequently, how these different woods and construction methods affect the overall sound.

Finally, but still crucially, we come to the bridge of the guitar. Beginner players must not underestimate just how important this block of wood is. It contains 6 pegs which are pulled out using special guitar pliers (or a 5-in-1 guitar key) when you change the strings on your instrument. Be delicate with the pegs and the bridge in general. Do not apply too much pressure on the area or try to change the setup. When in doubt, consult a professional at your local guitar store or at the very least, research what it is you are looking to do.

All in all, despite the elaboration on the different parts of the instrument and how to look after it, guitars are expensive pieces of equipment and deserve utmost respect. The life of a guitar depends on how you treat it both during and after playing.

One final piece of advice about mainte-nance is to use a dust cloth or specialised guitar cloth (with guitar conditioner if you can afford some) to clean your guitar at least once a month. Dust can damage the pickups of electric guitars and can age an acoustic guitar very badly.

READING TABS

The housekeeping is out of the way and you are ready to learn how to play guitar. In this section, we will be tackling chords but before getting into chord shapes and where to place your fingers, we need to address how guitarists read music.

```
E|—0———-|
B|—0———-|
G|—0———-|
D|—0———-|
A|—0———-|
E|—0———-|
```

This diagram above is a 'tab', short for tablature and it is what we use in guitar music to indicate where we should place our fingers and what note to play. The E at the top of the diagram is the high string of the guitar and the E at the bottom is the low E and so, tabs are read from the bottom up and not the top up. The number on the string indicates the fret we play on the fretboard. Therefore, a '0' indicates that we are to play an open string without pressing on the fretboard. The diagram above shows how we tune a guitar: by playing each string open to match the EADGBE standard tuning.

Another example:

```
E|—-———|
B|—-———-|
G|—-———-|
D|—3———-|
A|—3———-|
E|—1———-|
```

In the above diagram, we see that the G, B and high E strings are not in use so we DO NOT platy them. The chord above is called an F power chord which means it is a short version of the long F chord. This is our first chord.

Step 1: Place your index finger on the first fret of the low E string.

Step 2: Place your ring finger on the third fret of the A string.

Step 3: Place your pinky on the third fret of the D string.

Step 4: Strum (with your right hand) the top three strings being careful not to play the high three.

This is a power chord and the shape that your fingers are in can be transposed any-where on the fretboard to create different power chords, which are essential for riffs, which we will come to later.

Moving the same shape up from the first fret to the third fret creates a G power chord. It looks like this:

```
E|————|
B|————|
G|————|
D|-—5—|
A|—5—-|
E|—3—-|
```

An E power chord is:

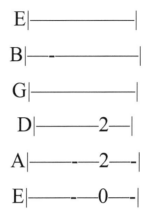

```
E|——————————|
B|——-———————|
G|——————————|
D|————2—|
A|———-—2—-|
E|———-—0—-|
```

An A power chord is:

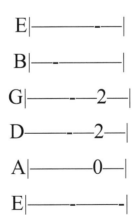

```
E|————-—|
B|——-———|
G|———-—2—|
D———-—2—|
A|————0—|
E|———-———-|
```

A B power chord is:

```
E|——————————|
B|——————————|
G|——-—4——————|
D|——-—4——————|
A|————-2————-|
E|——————————-—|
```

CHORD PROGRESSIONS

Let us slow things right down though. The reason I showed you power chords early on is because they are the easiest version of any chord you might need to use. But before taking another step, you need to learn the most basic chord progression which all beginner guitarist use: C, G, Am, F.

A chord progression is a series of (usually 3 or 4) chords which are played over and over in a song. Hundreds of thousands of pop and rock songs use the generic C, G, Am and F progression which is why it is essential to learn. Practice songs are included later on in the book so try to master this progression in this section before advancing to tackling anything more complex.

We are starting with a C major chord, or simply what we call 'C'. This going to be the basis for the entire exercise. It will take time and energy to master the progression itself so while I would usually say to focus on every chord individually, it is worth giving the entire progression a shot once you are somewhat comfortable with each chord.

The earlier on that you start practicing, the easier it will become.

C MAJOR CHORD

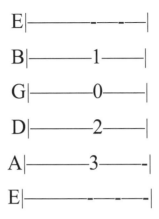

```
E|————-——|
B|———1———|
G|———0———|
D|———2———|
A|———3———-|
E|————-——-——|
```

Here we have the C chord. It looks daunting but one needn't worry because everything is explained step by step.

Step 1: You want to get your fingers in the right position so you can start to memorise the chord shapes. You will start by placing your ring finger (fourth finger) on the third fret of the A string.

Step 2: Next, put your middle finger on the second fret of the D string. I understand that this feels like a close tuck and it is. Therefore, really push down so that the notes can ring out when you strum later.

Step 3: Leaving the G string open and untouched (hence the 0 in the diagram), place your index (pointer) finger on the first fret of the B string.

This is the C major shape. Truth be told, it will feel uncomfortable and maybe even painful when you first become acquainted with this chord shape. But the practice pays off because after a while you will be able to do a C major chord shape without thinking twice. It's all about practice and muscle memory.

This is the first chord of the four chord sequence. Now, we must advance to the G major chord.

G MAJOR CHORD

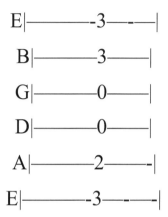

```
E|————-3—-—|
B|————3——|
G|————0——|
D|————0——|
A|————2——-|
E|————-3—-—-|
```

The G major chord is one of the reasons you should be learning guitar: in and of itself. It is wholesome, melodic and overall a gorgeous sounding chord.

Step 1: To start creating the shape, place your middle finger on the third fret of the low E string.

Step 2: Next, place your index finger on the second fret of the A string.

Step 3: Place your ring finger on the third fret of the B string and your pinky under it on the third fret of the high E string.

Once more, this position is not exactly the most fun for a beginner and it is a big jump from C to G. Nonetheless, it is a pivotal chord to learn for any genre of music. I urge you not to give up though, no matter how hard you find playing it. Perseverance is key.

A tip regarding this chord is that if you find the high notes difficult to keep down i.e. your ring and pinky on the B and E strings, then just try playing the top four strings and progressively introducing the high notes.

A MINOR CHORD

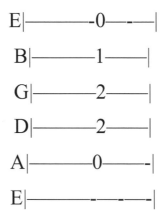

```
E|————-0——-—|
B|————1———|
G|————2———|
D|————2———|
A|————0———-|
E|————————-———-|
```

Every chord progression needs a good minor chord to bring it together. No chord does this more so than A minor. Unlike the other chords in this progression, this one does not use the low E string so when you play it, start out slow ensuring not to hit that low string.

Step 1: Place your middle finger on the second fret of the D string.

Step 2: Place your ring finger under it on the second fret of the G string.

Step 3: Finish the chord shape with your index finger on the first fret of the B string.

Step 4: Strum the chord using all strings except the low E.

F MAJOR CHORD

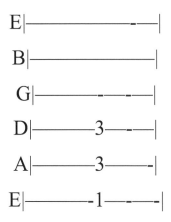

```
E|——————-—|
B|——————|
G|————-—-—|
D|———3—-—|
A|———3———-|
E|———-1—-——-|
```

The F major chord is by far the hardest chord that a beginner could come across. The full shape is found in the introduction of this book and if you feel brave enough, try tackling it. However, since this book is designed to get you under way on the guitar in a week, as a beginner, you need the simplified version.

We came across this exact version of F major earlier.

Step 1: Place your index finger on the first fret of the E string.

Step 2: Place your ring finger on the third fret of the A string.

Step 3: Place your ring finger on the third fret of the D string.

So now that you have the tools for your first chord progression, it's time for you to practice, practice, practice! Do not take another step until you have mastered each of the four chords and can comfortably change between them. Once you have nailed each chord, try playing them in this easy sequence:

C	C	C	C	G	G	G	G
Am	**Am**	**Am**	**Am**	**F**	**F**	**F**	**F**

The purpose of this exercise is to get you into a groove or rhythm of playing. It's one thing to learn to play the notes and another thing entirely to make it into music.

PICKING

What must be addressed is picking/strumming. Picking patterns are an essential part of playing the guitar and make riffs/chords sound either amazing or terrible. When starting out on guitar, most players pick downwards on every stroke. This works for some riffs but upstrokes are just as important. When writing out picking patterns, guitarists use D (down pick) and U (up pick) to signify what sort of picking is used. Try picking in alternate picking patterns like these:

D   D   U   D   D   U

In this picking pattern, you will pick the strings in a 'down, down, up' pattern i.e. two down picks and one up pick. This is a great beginner's pattern as it only involves one up pick.

D   U   D   D   U

Similar to the previous pattern, this one is slightly more challenging but you can master it with a bit of practice.

These are the primary two picking patterns used for playing chords and riffs. When you practice more and you get the hang of riffing, the picking pattern of a song will come naturally to you. The whole idea of a picking pattern is to make the riff run smoothly without breaks which can make a guitarist sound amateur and unprofessional. It's similar to a violinist who learns how to bow properly and fluidly.

Guitarists must learn as early as possible how to pick appropriately. On the occasion, you might find that some songs and riffs have multiple possibilities for picking patterns and there isn't only one right way of playing the song. This is fine too and in these cases, it is just a matter of what feels best for you.

Some songs start on an up-pick. While

rare, I would encourage you to practice any of the riffs in this book with an up-picked start. What happens when you try this is your muscle memory improves because you are taking on a technique which isn't natural. What *is* natural when you start playing a riff is to down pick from the start. Alternating shouldn't be a huge aspect of your practicing but it should be included nonetheless. You'll thank your future guitarist self for giving this a go earlier on in your musical career.

SWING LOW, SWEET CHARIOT

  C F C
Swing low, sweet chariot,

            G
Comin' for to carry me home.

    C   F   C
Swing low, sweet chariot,

        G C
Comin' for to carry me home.

  C   F   C
I looked over Jordan, and what did I see,

         G
Comin' for to carry me home.

  C   F C
A band of angels comin' after me,

```
        G    C
Comin' for to carry me home.

     C        F     C
If you get there before I do,

              G
Comin' for to carry me home.

   C                F   C
Just tell my friends that I'm a comin' too.

     G        C
Comin' for to carry me home.


   C          F      C
I'm sometimes up and sometimes down,


              G
Comin' for to carry me home.

   C           F    C
But still my soul feels heavenly bound.
```

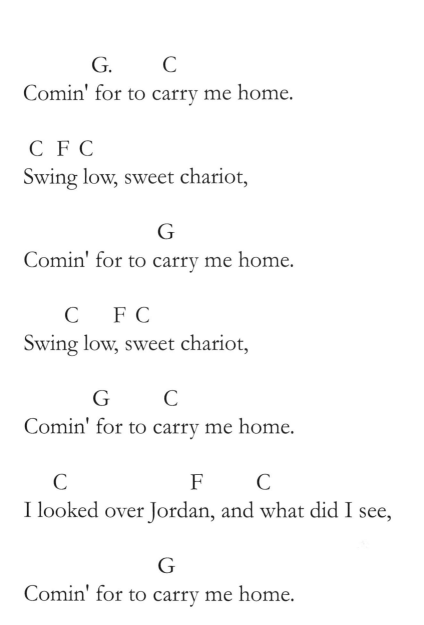

     G.   C
Comin' for to carry me home.

 C F C
Swing low, sweet chariot,

          G
Comin' for to carry me home.

    C   F C
Swing low, sweet chariot,

     G   C
Comin' for to carry me home.

   C   F   C
I looked over Jordan, and what did I see,

          G
Comin' for to carry me home.

   C   F   C
A band of angels comin' after me,

```
          G   C
Comin' for to carry me home.

     C        F      C
If you get there before I do,

               G
Comin' for to carry me home.

   C7                  F    C
Just tell my friends that I'm a comin' too.

     G   C
Comin' for to carry me home.


   C        F     C
I'm sometimes up and sometimes down,


               G
Comin' for to carry me home.

   C         F    C
But still my soul feels heavenly bound.
```

```
    G          C
Comin' for to carry me home.
```

THIS LITTLE LIGHT OF MINE

G
This little light of mine, I'm gonna let it shine

C   G
This little light of mine, I'm gonna let it shine

                                     Em
This little light of mine, I'm gonna let it shine

   G   D   G
Let it shine, let it shine, let it shine.

G
Hide it under a bushel, no! I'm gonna let it shine

C   G
Hide it under a bushel, no! I'm gonna let it shine

                                   Em
Hide it under a bushel, no! I'm gonna let it shine

```
   G           D          G
Let it shine, let it shine, let it shine.
```

```
G
Don't let Satan blow it out, I'm gonna let it
shine
```

```
C                                G
Don't let Satan blow it out, I'm gonna let it
shine
```

```
                              Em
Don't let Satan blow it out, I'm gonna let it
shine
```

```
     G          D         G
Let it shine, let it shine, let it shine.
```

```
G
Let it shine till Jesus comes, I'm gonna let it
shine
```

```
C                                G
Let it shine till Jesus comes, I'm gonna let it
shine
```

                                   Em

Let it shine till Jesus comes, I'm gonna let it shine

           G   D   G

Let it shine, let it shine, let it shine.

I'LL FLY AWAY

G   G   C   G

Some glad morning when this life is o'er, I'll fly away

G   D G

To a home on God's celestial shore, I'll fly away

G   G C   G

I'll fly away, O glory, I'll fly away

G C G   D G

When I die, hallelujah, by and by I'll fly away

G   G   C   G

When the shadows of this life have grown, I'll fly away

```
G                              D   G
Like a bird from prison bars has flown, I'll fly
away


G          G    C    G
I'll fly away, O glory, I'll fly away

G  C G                 D   G
When I die, hallelujah, by and by I'll fly away


G          G          C    G
Just a few more weary days, and then, I'll fly
away

G                      D   G
To a land where joys shall never end, I'll fly
away


G          G    C    G
I'll fly away, O glory, I'll fly away
```

```
G   C G                 D G
When I die, hallelujah, by and by I'll fly away.

G           G           C    G
Some glad morning when this life is o'er, I'll
fly away

G                       D7  G
To a home on God's celestial shore, I'll fly
away



G           G   C   G
I'll fly away, O glory, I'll fly away

G   C G                 D  G
When I die, hallelujah, by and by I'll fly away

G           G           C    G
When the shadows of this life have grown, I'll
fly away
```

```
G                              D   G
Like a bird from prison bars has flown, I'll fly
away


G           G    C    G
I'll fly away, O glory, I'll fly away

G   C G                  D   G
When I die, hallelujah, by and by I'll fly away


G           G           C    G
Just a few more weary days, and then, I'll fly
away

G                              D   G
To a land where joys shall never end, I'll fly
away


G           G    C    G
I'll fly away, O glory, I'll fly away
```

```
G   C G                    D  G
```
When I die, hallelujah, by and by I'll fly away.

DANNY BOY

     C   F
Oh Danny boy,   the pipes, the pipes are calling

        C   Am   G
From glen to glen and down the mountain
side

        C   F
The summer's gone and all the roses falling

       C Am   G   C
'Tis you, 'tis you   must go and I must bide

G Am   F   C
But come ye   back when summer's in the
meadow

G Am   Am   F   C   G
Or when the valley's hushed and white with

snow

     C   F   C Am   G   F
And I'll be here in sunshine or in shadow

     C   Am Dm G   C
Oh Danny boy, oh Danny boy I love you so

      C   F
But if he come and all the roses dying

    C   Am   G   G
And I am dead, as dead I well may be

       C   F F
You'll come and find the place where I am ly-
ing

     C Am F G   C
And kneel and say   an Ave there for me

```
G Am      C        F          C
```
And I shall feel, though soft you tread above me

```
G Am  Am    F      C      G
```
And then my grave will richer, sweeter be

```
G  Am    C   C          C
```
For you will bend and tell me that you love me

```
        C      Am         G     C  G
```
And I shall rest in peace until you come to me

```
        C      Am      C   G        C
```
And I shall rest in peace until you come to me.

DRUNKEN SAILOR

Am
What shall we do with the drunken sailor?

G
What shall we do with the drunken sailor?

Am
What shall we do with the drunken sailor?

Am G   Am
Ear-ly in the morning

Am
Hooray, and up she rises

G
Hooray, and up she rises

Am
Hooray, and up she rises

Am G   Am
Ear-ly in the morning

Am
Put him in the long boat 'til he's sober

G
Put him in the long boat 'til he's sober

Am
Put him in the long boat 'til he's sober

Am   G   Am
Ear-ly in the morning

Am
Pull out the plug and wet him all over

G
Pull out the plug and wet him all over

Am
Pull out the plug and wet him all over

Am   G   Am
Ear-ly in the morning

Am
Put him in the bilge and make him drink it

G
Put him in the bilge and make him drink it

Am
Put him in the bilge and make him drink it

Am   G   Am
Ear-ly in the morning

Am
Put him in a leaky boat and make him bale her

G
Put him in a leaky boat and make him bale her

Am
Put him in a leaky boat and make him bale her

```
Am        G        Am
```
Ear-ly in the morning

```
Am
```
Tie him to the scuppers with the hose pipe on
him

```
G
```
Tie him to the scuppers with the hose pipe on
him

```
Am
```
Tie him to the scuppers with the hose pipe on
him

```
Am        G        Am
```
Ear-ly in the morning.

AMERICA THE BEAUTIFUL

    G   D
O beautiful for spacious skies,

    D   G
for amber waves of grain

             D
For purple mountain majesties,

  A   A   D D
above the fruited plain!

  G   D
America! America!

    D   G
God shed his grace on thee

    C   G
And crown thy good with brotherhood,

    C   D   G
from sea to shining sea!

```
 G          D
O beautiful for pilgrim feet,

   D             G
whose stern impassioned stress

              D
A thoroughfare of freedom beat,

 A       A  D
across the wilderness!

 G     D
America! America!

   D          G
God mend thine every flaw

   C          G
Confirm thy soul in self-control,

   C    D  G
Thy liberty in law!
```

```
 G        D
```
O beautiful for heroes proved,

```
 D      G
```
in liberating strife.

```
                D
```
Who more than self their country loved,

```
 A    A     D  D
```
and mercy more than life!

```
 G     D
```
America! America!

```
 D        G
```
May God thy gold refine

```
  C         G
```
Till all success be nobleness,

```
  C    D   G
```
and every gain divine!

```
    G       D
O beautiful for patriot dream,

     D          G
that sees beyond the years

             D
Thine alabaster cities gleam,

   A      A   D   D
undimmed by human tears!

  G     D
America! America!

    D           G
God shed his grace on thee

     C             G
And crown thy good with brotherhood,

     C    D    G
from sea to shining sea!
```

```
  G        D
O beautiful for halcyon skies,

  D        G
For amber waves of grain,

         D
For purple mountain majesties

  A     A   D   D
Above the enamelled plain!

  G    D
America! America!

  D          G
God shed his grace on thee

   C          G
Till souls wax fair as earth and air

   C   D   G
And music-hearted sea!
```

```
  G        D
O beautiful for pilgrims feet,

   D          G
Whose stem impassioned stress

              D
A thoroughfare for freedom beat

 A      A   D  D
Across the wilderness!

 G     D
America! America!

   D         G
God shed his grace on thee

   C               G
Till paths be wrought through wilds of
thought

   C    D   G
By pilgrim foot and knee!
```

```
G         D
```
O beautiful for glory-tale

```
 D      G
```
Of liberating strife

```
              D
```
When once and twice, for man's avail

```
 A      A    D    D
```
Men lavished precious life!

```
G     D
```
America! America!

```
 D           G
```
God shed his grace on thee

```
  C           G
```
Till selfish gain no longer stain

```
  C    D    G
```
The banner of the free!

```
  G        D
O beautiful for patriot dream

   D        G
That sees beyond the years

           D
Thine alabaster cities gleam

  A     A  D   D
Undimmed by human tears!

  G    D
America! America!

   D         G
God shed his grace on thee

   C          G
Till nobler men keep once again

   C    D  G
Thy whiter jubilee!
```

G   D

O beautiful for spacious skies,

   D   G

for amber waves of grain

              D

For purple mountain majesties,

A   A   D   D

above the fruited plain!

G   D

America! America!

   D   G

God shed his grace on thee

   C   G

And crown thy good with brotherhood,

   C   D   G

from sea to shining sea!

HOME ON THE RANGE

G   C
Oh give me a home where the buffalo roam

    G   D
Where the deer and the antelope play

  G   C
Where seldom is heard a discouraging word

    G   D   G
And the skies are not cloudy all day

  D   G
Home home on the range

                  D
Where the deer and the antelope play

    G   C
Where seldom is heard a discouraging word

```
    G        D      G
And the skies are not cloudy all day


G                       C
The Red Man was pressed from this part of
the west

       G            D
It's not likely he'll ever return

     G              C
To the banks of Red River where seldom if
ever

    G      D        G
His flickering campfires still burn


D       G
Home home on the range

                    D
Where the deer and the antelope play
```

```
   G              C
Where seldom is heard a discouraging word

    G         D       G
And the skies are not cloudy all day


G                      C
How often at night when the heavens are
bright

     G                      D
With the light from the glittering stars

    G                   C
Have I stood there amazed and asked as I
gazed

     G     D        G
If their glory exceeds that of ours
```

```
D          G
Home home on the range

                    D
Where the deer and the antelope play

     G          C
Where seldom is heard a discouraging word

      G      D      G
And the skies are not cloudy all day


G                      C
Oh give me a land where the bright diamond
sand

     G          D
Flows leisurely down the stream

        G              C
Where the graceful white swan goes gliding
along
```

```
   G     D    G
Like a maid in a heavenly dream


D          G
Home home on the range

                   D
Where the deer and the antelope play

   G          C
Where seldom is heard a discouraging word

   G      D     G
And the skies are not cloudy all day

   G      D     G
And the skies are not cloudy all day.
```

I'VE GOT PEACE LIKE A RIVER

     G   C

I've got peace like a river

     G   D

I've got peace like a river

     G   C   D

I've got peace like a river in my soul

     G   C

I've got peace like a river

     G   D

I've got peace like a river

     G   C   D   G

I've got peace like a river in my soul

     G   C

I've got joy like a fountain

```
      G          D
I've got joy like a fountain

       G          C         D
I've got joy like a fountain in my soul

       G          C
I've got joy like a fountain

       G          D
I've got joy like a fountain

       G          C   D   G
I've got joy like a fountain in my soul


       G          C
I've got love like an ocean

       G          D
I've got love like an ocean

       G          C         D
I've got love like an ocean in my soul
```

```
    G          C
I've got love like an ocean

     G          D
I've got love like an ocean

     G          C   D   G
I've got love like an ocean in my soul.

    G          C
I've got peace like a river

     G          D
I've got peace like a river

     G          C          D
I've got peace like a river in my soul

     G          C
I've got peace like a river

     G          D
I've got peace like a river
```

```
        G          C    D    G
I've got peace like a river in my soul


        G              C
I've got joy like a fountain

        G          D
I've got joy like a fountain


        G          C         D
I've got joy like a fountain in my soul

        G          C
I've got joy like a fountain

        G          D
I've got joy like a fountain

        G          C    D    G
I've got joy like a fountain in my soul
```

```
  G         C
I've got love like an ocean

    G           D
I've got love like an ocean

    G       C       D
I've got love like an ocean in my soul

    G         C
I've got love like an ocean

    G         D
I've got love like an ocean

    G         C   D   G
I've got love like an ocean in my soul.
```

BLUE CHRISTMAS

    C   G

I have a blue Christmas without you

     G   C

I'll be so blue just thinking about you

   C   C   F

Decorations of red, on a green Christmas tree

D   G

won't be the same dear, if you're not here
with me.

       C   G

And when those blue snow flakes start falling,

     G   C

that's when those blue memories start calling,

    C   C   F   F

you'll be doing alright, with your Christmas of
white,

```
 G          C
but I'll have a blue blue Christmas.


         C          G
Oh, oh, ohh Ah   Ah    ah ah ahh ohhhh

        G          C
ohh, ohh, ohh Ahhhhh Ahh ahh a ahh ohhhh

        C     C        F
You'll be doing alright with your Christmas of
white

   G          C
but I'll have a blue blue Christmas.
```

DECK THE HALLS

C   Am   G C
Deck the hall with boughs of holly,

G   C   Am G C
Fa la la la la la la la la.

 C   Am G C
'Tis the season to be jolly,

G   C   Am G C
Fa la la la la la la la la.

G   C   G
Don we now our gay apparel

C   Am   D   G
Fa la la la la la la la la.

C   Am   G C
Troll the ancient Christmas carol,

F   C   Am G C
Fa la la la la la la la la.

```
F    C    Am    G    C
```

```
C          Am G C
```
See the blazing yule before us,

```
G     C  Am G C
```
Fa la la la la la la la la.

```
C          Am G  C
```
Strike the harp and join the chorus.

```
G     C  Am G C
```
Fa la la la la la la la la.

```
G     C    G
```
Follow me in merry measure,

```
C    Am    D  G
```
Fa la la la la la la la la.

```
C          Am  G  C
```
While I tell of Christmas treasure,

```
F       C   Am G C
```
Fa la la la la la la la la.

```
F   C     Am     G     C
```

```
C        Am G   C
```
Fast away the old year passes,

```
G       C   Am G C
```
Fa la la la la la la la la.

```
C           Am   G   C
```
Hail the new, ye lads and lasses!

```
G       C   Am G C
```
Fa la la la la la la la la.

```
G         C   G
```
Sing we joyous all together,

```
C   Am     D   G
```
Fa la la la la la la la la.

```
C          Am  G  C
Heedless of the wind and weather,

F       C   Am  G  C
Fa la la la la la la la la.

F    C    Am     G     C
```

AMAZING GRACE

```
C   C   F   C
```
Amazing grace How sweet the sound

```
  C           G   G
```
That saved a wretch like me!

```
  C    C   F   C
```
I once was lost, but now am found;

```
  C     G   C F C
```
Was blind, but now I see.

```
    C     C   F    C
```
'Twas grace that taught my heart to fear,

```
  C       G   G
```
And grace my fears relieved;

```
  C    C   F    C
```
How precious did that grace appear

```
  C   G   C F C
```
The hour I first believed.

```
      C   C      F      C
Through many dangers, toils and snares,

  C      G   G
I have already come;

    C      C      F      C
'Tis grace hath brought me safe thus far,

  C      G      C F C
And grace will lead me home.

  C      C      F      C
The Lord has promised good to me,

  C         G   G
His Word my hope secures;

  C      C      F      C
He will my Shield and Portion be,

  C   G      C F C
As long as life endures.
```

```
      C     C    F     C
Yea, when this flesh and heart shall fail,

   C           G    G
And mortal life shall cease,

  C     C    F   C
I shall possess, within the veil,

  C    G    C   C    D
A life of joy and peace


     C       C    F      C
The earth shall soon dissolve like snow,

   C           G    G
The sun forbears to shine;

   C     C    F    C
But God, who called me here below,

   C   G   C  F  C
Will be forever mine.
```

```
     C       C      F       C
When we've been there ten thousand years,

      C          G  G
Bright shining as the sun,

     C     C     F       C
We've no less days to sing God's praise

     C     G     C   F C
Than when we'd first begun.
```

BE THOU MY VISION

C   Am   F   G   C
Be Thou my vision, O Lord of my heart;

G   Am   F   C G
Naught be all else to me, save that Thou art-

Am   G F   C   G F G
Thou my best thought, by day or by night,

C   Am   F   G C
Waking or sleeping, Thy presence my Light.

C   Am   F   G C
Be Thou my Wisdom, and Thou my true
Word;

G   Am   F   C G
I ever with Thee, and Thou with me, Lord;

Am   G F   C G F G
Thou my great Father, I Thy true son,

```
C      Am        F    G   C
```
Thou in me dwelling, and I with Thee one.

```
C      Am        F    G   C
```
Riches I heed not, nor man's empty praise,

```
G      Am        F      C  G
```
Thou mine inheritance, now and al-ways;

```
Am     G   F   C      G  F  G
```
Thou and Thou only, first in my heart,

```
C         Am       F      G    C
```
High King of heaven, my Treasure Thou art.

```
C         Am       F    G   C
```
High King of heaven, my victory won,

```
G      Am          F      C      G
```
May I reach heaven's joys, O bright heav'n's
Sun!

```
Am     G  F        C   G  F  G
```
Heart of my own heart, whatever befall,

```
C        Am      F    G  C
```
Still be my vision, O Ruler of all.

HERE I AM LORD

G   Em   Am   Em Am   D
I, the Lord of sea and sky, I have heard my

people cry

G   Em   C   Am   D
All who dwell in dark and sin, My hand will

save.

G   Em   G   Em   Am   D
I who made the stars of night, I will make

their darkness bright.

G   Em   C   Am   D
Who will bear my light to them? Whom shall

I send?

G Em Am D G Em Am
Here I am Lord, Is it I Lord?

D   G Em   C Am   D
I have heard you calling in the night.

      G Em Am D   G Em Am
I will go Lord, If you lead me.

D   G Em   Am D   G Em Am D
I will hold your people in my hand.

G   Em   Am   D Am   D
I the Lord of snow and rain, I have borne my

peoples' pain.

G   Em   C   Am   D
I have wept for love of them...they turn away.

G   Em   D G   Em   Am   D
I will break their hearts of stone, Give them

hearts for love alone

```
G      Em   C   Am              D
```
I will speak my words to them, Whom shall I

```
 send?
```

```
G   Em  Am  D   G   Em  Am
```
Here I am Lord, Is it I Lord?

```
D      G   Em   C   Am      D
```
I have heard you calling in the night.

```
G   Em  Am  D    G   Em   Am
```
I will go Lord, If you lead me.

```
D      G   Em     G   Em   Am  D
```
I will hold your people in my hand.

```
G      Em    G    Em     Am      D
```
I the Lord of wind and flame, I will tend the

```
poor and lame.
```

```
G      Em   C    Am              D
```
I will set a feast for them. My hand will save.

G　　Em　　G　　Em　　Am　　D
Finest bread I will provide, 'til their hearts by

satisfied.

G　　Em　　C　　Am　　　　D
I will give my life to them.　Whom shall I

send?

G　Em Am D　G　Em　Am
Here I am Lord, Is it I Lord?

D　　G　Em　C　Am　　D
I have heard you calling in the night.

　G　Em Am D　　G　Em　Am
I will go Lord, If you lead me.

D　　G　Em　Am　D　G　Em Am D
I will hold your people in my hand.

G　Em Am D　G　Em　Am
Here I am Lord, Is it I Lord?

D   G Em   C Am   D

I have heard you calling in the night.

 G Em Am D   G Em Am

I will go Lord, If you lead me.

D   G Em   Am D   G Em Am D

I will hold your people in my hand.

—

65842171R00071

Made in the USA
Columbia, SC
14 July 2019